Angels of Great Joy

God's Messengers of the Nativity

Angels of Great Joy: God's Messengers of the Nativity

ISBN-10: 0-9860244-1-4
ISBN-13: 978-0-9860244-1-2

Edited by Jessa Sexton and Ashley Balding
Cover design and interior layout by Brianna Miele

Published by:
O'More Publishing
A Division of O'More College of Design
423 South Margin St.
Franklin, TN 37064 U.S.A.

Angels of Great Joy

God's Messengers of the Nativity

Contents

Angels in the Bible

Angels are mentioned many times in the New Testament as they are in the Old Testament. In the New Testament Jesus Christ validates their importance and existence. John M. Wilson in writing in the *International Standard Bible Encyclopedia* comments on the certainty of Jesus accepting the teaching about angels and the agreement that He taught of their existence, reality, and activity.1

The Greek word for angel is *aggelos*, meaning, in the original language, an agent or emissary intent on doing the will of God. In the New Testament both good and evil angels are mentioned. Colossians 2:15 records the triumph of Jesus Christ over certain angels called *archai* or principalities and over *dunaneis* or powers. Fallen angels are mentioned in 2 Peter 2:4. But by and large the angels of the New Testament assist the human race, and Christians in particular. Wilson concludes that angels watch over humanity and rejoice in the salvation of the human race. They can be regarded as ministering spirits for those who will inherit salvation.2

The acclaimed academician Carl Braaten hails the triumph of angels over evil forces. Braaten recognizes the cosmic struggle fought out on the planet Earth. We as Christians will not fight the battle alone just as Michael and other angels wage war against the Dragon in the Book of Revelation. "What is going on is happening on two levels. The heavenly and earthly levels of reality are interconnected." 3

God created angels for a purpose in this cosmic struggle. Mike Aquilina in his book, *Angels of God*, further observes that angels continue as our guardians and guides. They bring messages from heaven to Earth. As guardians, their main task has always been to get us to heaven, not necessarily to keep us from suffering or death. "We also tend to behave better when we know someone is watching. Our angels are always watching." 4

As previously mentioned, angels have always been present on the pages of the Old and New Testaments. Herbert Lockyer calculates that some form of the word *angel* appears in thirty-four different books of the Bible. They have their individual missions to perform and use their unique abilities. They have been employed in numberless ways as the messengers of God to men.5 However, angels have their limitations and certainly are not to be worshipped. As Billy Graham emphasizes, "We are not to pray to angels. Only the triune God is to be the object of our worship and our prayer." 6 The Apostle Paul observed that believers will judge certain angels (1 Corinthians 6:3). Jesus on one occasion told His listeners that in the afterlife believers will be like angels (Matthew 22:30).

The New Testament begins with an explosion of these heavenly messengers—angels of joy with glorious announcements. The nativity or announcement of the birth of Jesus Christ can be found in two of the four Gospels: Matthew and Luke. Angels announced the birth and parts of the infancy narrative. These announcements came to the humble of spirit. As the scholar Leon Morris writes in reference to Luke's Gospel, "As God worked out that great redemptive purpose Luke saw him as concerned with individual people. He did not see the divine purpose as appearing only in great movements of nations and peoples: it operated in the lives of humble men and women, for even the little people matter to God." 7

Gabriel Appears to Zechariah

Luke 1:1–25, 57–80

Luke's Gospel has been dated from the angel Gabriel's appearance to a country priest named Zechariah.

Zechariah was married to Elizabeth who was a priest's daughter. They were a very godly family. Luke described them as good people who pleased God and were obedient to His commandments. In many respects they were similar to a rural minister and his wife in more modern society. However, there was an overwhelming problem in this family: they had no children.

In ancient times childlessness was a stigma. Many in that time blamed lack of children on some type of sin or curse. In the Old Testament there are many examples of this social stigma. Hannah was taunted until God blessed her with a son by the name of Samuel. Rachel was ridiculed for being childless by Leah, the other wife of the patriarch Jacob. Sarah used a surrogate mother by the name of Hagar so that her husband Abraham could have a family. Biological progeny was much more important at that time than today when other options for having children have become available. Elizabeth made the comment in Luke's Gospel after her pregnancy, "What the Lord has done for me will keep people from looking down on me" (Luke 1:25).

The angel by the name of Gabriel made the announcement, not to Elizabeth, but to her husband Zechariah about the pregnancy. Zechariah had been bestowed a very special honor prior to this announcement. He had been selected to serve God by ministering in the Temple at Jerusalem. Morris mentions that there were many priests and not enough sacred duties for them all, so lots were cast to see who would perform each function. The offering of incense was regarded as a great privilege. A priest could not offer incense more than once in his entire lifetime (Mishnah, Tamid 5:2), and some priests never received that privilege. For Zechariah the offering would be the most honored time in his entire life. 8

Zechariah must have been tense as he entered the most holy place of the Temple. He had to make sure the priestly ritual was performed in dignity and precision before God. The people waiting on the outside were probably from his synagogue. Then the unthinkable happened. An angel of the Lord appeared to him. The Gospel of Luke describes Zechariah as confused and afraid. This type of language is often used to describe a reaction to angels. Angels are immediately recognized as imposing beings and not ordinary humans.

The angel, who had not yet introduced himself to Zechariah, told the country priest that his prayers had been answered. Speculation could be made about the kind of prayers uttered by Zechariah. He would not interject personal requests into prayers during a worship occasion. Unlike many ministers of today, personal references to family matters were not the subject of priestly speech. Was Zechariah praying for the spiritual health of Israel? He had witnessed the secular ways of the big cities and the money-loving priesthood. In any event, what he heard from the angel was mind-boggling.

The appearance of the angel immediately created fear, or

phobus. The Greek word *phobus* is the usual word for fear and the word that became the root of the English word phobia. But the angel calmed Zechariah and told him not to be afraid. The angel promised him joy of the highest kind. *The Expositors Greek Testament* describes the joy of a son late born and of a special nature.9 This promise overwhelmed the priest. He had hoped for a son and an heir. He immediately began to rationalize the situation. How could he know that this would happen? He and his wife were old, and children were not born to the elderly. These questions were natural and were not sinful comments in themselves. Finally, Zechariah asked for a heavenly sign, and the angel complied. At this point, detecting doubt on the part of the priest, the angel identified himself as Gabriel and told Zechariah that his priestly voice would be silenced until the birth of his promised son.

Meanwhile, the crowd, which was made up of his synagogue congregation, continued to wait for the priest. These people must have wondered many things as they waited outside. And when Zechariah emerged from the temple, they soon discovered that he could not speak. They also suspected that something most unusual had happened. Zechariah had been confused and terrified in the presence of Gabriel. Now the priest was confident, for God had given him a sign that he humbly accepted. The time for the birth of a son had been revealed to him, and he wrote on a tablet that the child's name would be John. The name John went against all family tradition, but Zechariah was adamant as he remembered the words of Gabriel. His resolution and obedience were rewarded with the restored power of speech after John was born. As he began to speak, he immediately praised God.

The Gospel of Luke records the song of praise from the lips of Zechariah. He saw in all of this the plan of God to save His people. Leon Morris comments that Zechariah's song of praise surprises us by not beginning with John but with the Messiah who was about to be sent.10 The song of praise revealed the role of John as the Baptist who would be the prophet of the Most High, an honor not given for many centuries. But John the Baptist would be a forerunner to prepare the way for the Messiah. This John would call all people to repentance and tell them about the Messiah.

Throughout Zechariah's encounter with Gabriel, the word *joy* is emphasized. The Bible says the priest will be proud of his son the prophet. His son will be filled with the Holy Spirit. John will be filled with special powers from his birth, and he will be great, yet in subjection to a Greater One. John will change the thoughts of his countrymen, and the patriarchs will be pleased. Morris' comments have much significance: "The fathers may mean the patriarchs, the great ancestors of the present sinners. From their vantage point in the next world they looked at their descendants and were displeased. But John would bring about such a change that the fathers would come to look with favour on Israel. The result would be a people prepared for the Lord."11

The angel brought joy to the priest and his wife Elizabeth. He gave the priest an extraordinary sign of silence—silence in which he could reflect upon this most extraordinary announcement. This news would later be called "good news "and would climax in the announcement of the birth of the Messiah.

Gabriel Appears to Mary

Luke 1:26–56; Matthew 1:18–25

The angel Gabriel is quite present in Luke's Gospel. After his appearance to Zechariah, he appeared to a young woman by the name of Mary, or Miriam in the Aramaic dialect. Mary eventually became one of the most prominent women in the Bible, but her beginnings were very humble. The name Mary was common in the New Testament, occurring fifty-one times. There were several women by the name of Mary mentioned in the scriptures including Mary, the Virgin; Mary of Magdala; and Mary of Bethany.

This Mary, a young woman and a virgin, was of particular interest to the writer Luke who might have conversed with her at a later time during his careful research of the incidents that appear in his Gospel. Louis Sweet comments in the *International Standard Bible Encyclopedia* about Luke's Gospel presenting Mary's deep and personal expressions including her call, her fears, her loyal submission, and her sacred and unselfish joy. On the other hand, the Gospel of Matthew tells of the outward and public expressions of Mary such as the shame and suspicion that fell upon her, her bitter humiliation, and her ultimate vindication. From the two Gospel narratives we have an interesting biography. She is shown as complex and contemplative throughout the New Testament. Her greatest life experience, God dwelling among humans, began with the appearance of Gabriel to her as a young peasant woman. 12

Gabriel appeared to Mary in her hometown of Nazareth. Nazareth in those days was a small, unimportant village. The expression "can anything good come from Nazareth?" is written in the scriptures (John 1:46). Nazareth's religious beliefs were conservative and its spiritual leaders unreceptive towards Jesus in His ministry. Despite the town's shortcomings, God found the best of females for His divine plan. This young woman, probably still in her teens, was selected to be the mother of the Messiah, the Son of God. Thus Gabriel was delivering an awesome and unique message to Mary of Nazareth.

The visit of the angel caused Mary to be troubled. Luke uses the same word for troubled as he did to describe Zechariah's reaction to the angel. Luke notes that Mary was engaged to Joseph who was from the family of King David. Engagement was a very serious contract in that time and not easily broken. Gabriel greeted Mary with great words of praise. Mary was truly blessed, and the Lord was with her. Mary would not forget these words when she sang her hymn of praise. The appearances of Gabriel to Zechariah and Mary were similar in that both realized great blessings were bestowed upon them. Both were deeply troubled and afraid in the presence of Gabriel. Gabriel calmed them with the words of his message.

Mary listened to the words of Gabriel as Zechariah had listened earlier. Gabriel brought a message of great joy and promise. Mary, unlike Zechariah, believed without a heavenly sign or wonder. She heard Gabriel talk about a son who would be called Jesus. This Jesus was to be great and called the Son of God Most High. Jesus would be a king as His ancestor

David was king. Jesus would rule the people of Israel forever, and His kingdom would never end.

Mary continued to be puzzled, as any woman would be who heard such news. She accepted the promises of greatness for Jesus but knew that conception was impossible in her present circumstances. She had promised to have no sexual relationship with a man till her marriage. Gabriel assured her that the conception would occur through the power of the Most High. What Mary comprehended in this most unique of Gabriel's appearances cannot be known. She might have thought that she would be the mother of a great king who would rule Israel. The bloodline of Mary went back to David, as Luke records in chapter three of his Gospel. Mary likely confined her aspirations for her son to the boundaries of her own people. This indeed would be a high honor. She had asked only one question, "How can this happen? I am not married?" (Luke 1:24). Mary's character was revealed in her moral life. Chaste women did not have children unless married.

At a later point in the conversation, Gabriel emphasized that Mary's son would be called the holy Son of God. Gabriel, knowing that Mary remained confused, gave her an example of God's power and mentioned her relative Elizabeth who was now six months pregnant. Gabriel then spoke words similar to words spoken to Sarah in the Old Testament, "Nothing is impossible for God" (Luke 1:37; Genesis 18:14).

Before an examination of Mary's visit to Elizabeth will be examined, Mary's reaction to Gabriel's message must be evaluated. Her heroism cannot be underestimated. As Leon Morris concludes, "Mary's response is one of quiet submission. Handmaid (*doule*) means slave girl; it expresses complete obedience. The slave girl could not but do the will of her master." This is reinforced with Mary's expression in her view towards God as her Master; "let it be according to your word" (Luke 1:38).

We sometimes miss Mary's quiet heroism. She was not yet married to Joseph. She could expect a strong reaction from Joseph to her pregnancy, and Matthew tells us that he did in fact think of divorcing her (1:19). Again, while the death penalty for adultery did not seem to have been carried out often, it was still an option. Mary knew the potential for suffering, even for death. But she recognized the will of God and accepted it. 13

Mary Visits Elizabeth

Luke 1:39–56

Mary's reaction to Gabriel's message was one of action. Morris observes that she lost no time in paying a visit to her relative Elizabeth. In mathematical terms Mary visited Elizabeth in the sixth month of Elizabeth's pregnancy. Opinions vary as to whether she stayed for the birth of John, but in all likelihood she remained with Elizabeth and her husband Zechariah for this great event. 14

It would be pure guesswork as to when Mary informed Joseph of her condition. Matthew's Gospel simply states that "a young woman named Mary was engaged to Joseph from King David's family. But before they were married, she learned that she was going to have a baby by God's Holy Spirit" (1:18). Matthew does not tell when the news was broken to Joseph. When Joseph found out, he considered his options. In his commentary on Matthew, Alfred Plummer writes, "The two narratives are wholly independent, as their great differences show. These differences do not amount to contradictions, though we do not know how to harmonize them." Plummer concludes that certain details are impossible to completely ascertain. 15

It is certain that after Gabriel informed Mary of the virgin birth, she quickly planned her visit to Elizabeth, probably both for comfort and assurance. Logical thinking and future examination of Mary's character reveals a young woman who pondered or thought deeply. This would make the visit to Elizabeth very crucial. Elizabeth's counsel would be invaluable to Mary. After all, Mary knew that Elizabeth had received the blessing and the favor of God, or *Yahweh.* If the visit lasted the probable last three months of Elizabeth's pregnancy, Mary must have received much comfort and blessing during this time.

This visit probably began as a spontaneous trip from Nazareth to a town in the hill country of Judea, another rural setting. Their initial greeting reinforced Mary's belief that her child would be very special. Elizabeth greeted Mary with great excitement for she felt her own baby leap inside of her. Luke further adds that the Holy Spirit helped Elizabeth interpret the meaning of Mary's baby. Thus Mary who came to praise Elizabeth was herself the object of praise. Elizabeth recognized that Mary was blessed among all women. She was not competing with Mary, but she was acknowledging the superiority of Mary's blessing. Mary's child would be the Messiah. Morris comments that there was an absence of jealousy on the part of Elizabeth. She was the older woman but in genuine humility recognized the greater blessing God had given Mary. "A further point of interest is that John the Baptist did not recognize Jesus as Messiah until the baptism. Apparently Elizabeth's recognition that he is Lord was inspired, but personal. John had to find it out for himself."16

Mary's Song of Praise

Luke 1:46–56

The song of praise that Mary sang is recorded in Luke. Luke, as stated, was most likely able to interview Mary in her later years, and Mary recalled the song. The song has been called the Magnificat, meaning song of praise. When Mary composed the song has remained a matter of supposition. She may have on her travel to Elizabeth's home or while staying with her. The song expresses her love and devotion to God, or *Yahweh*, and can be divided into sections.

The first part of the song is Mary's own personal gratitude to God for blessing her. She expressed her feelings in the most humble of terms: "God cares for me His humble servant" (Luke 1:48). The feminine word for servant in Greek (*doule*), as previously mentioned, literally meant slave. She pictured herself as a slave who, somehow in the great plan of God, was exceedingly blessed. Mary then expanded this song of praise to include mercy towards everyone who worshipped Him. The expression, God all Powerful, was a particularly strong acknowledgment of the might of *Yahweh*. She echoed the sentiments of Gabriel that nothing was impossible for God! Mary's reply to Gabriel was, "I am the Lord's servant (*doule*). Let it happen as you have said" (Luke 1:38).

Mary then expanded her song proclaiming the greatness of God in ruling this world: "The Lord has used His powerful arm to scatter those who are proud. God drags strong rulers from their thrones and put humble people in places of power. God gives the hungry good things to eat, and sends the rich away with nothing. God helps His servant Israel and is always merciful to His people. The Lord made this promise to our ancestors, to Abraham and his family forever!"(Luke 1:51–55).

The completion of the song reversed the prevailing idea of the social status of humanity. The humble would be exalted while the Lord scattered the proud and overturned rulers. God would feed those in need and would send the wealthy away with nothing. Mary believed that this revelation would exalt her nation Israel. Salvation for others had not entered her thought at this time. Many commentators have thought that the song was modeled on Hannah's song from the Old Testament. One comments, "The hymn modeled in part on that of Hannah in I Samuel 2:1, is peculiarly suitable to the circumstances of Mary, and plainly could not have been composed after the resurrection of Christ." 17

Mary Considered

Louis Sweet characterizes Mary in this way: a typical Jewish believer of the best sort. She was deeply pensive and meditative but not a daring thinker. Her inherited Messianic beliefs could not prepare her for the method in which Jesus became involved in the world in such an unexpected and new way. 18 *Time Magazine* in the March 21, 2005, edition talks about the controversy Mary continues to generate: "Mary was not always such a lightning rod. Early on, Christians rallied around her importance. The Council of Ephesus in 431 affirmed her to be the *Theotikos* or Mother of God. Admittedly the move was less about her than him. It repudiated a specific heresy—that Mary's son and the Messiah were two different beings—and it made the Incarnation much more immediate." The article mentions that Martin Luther was "fond of Mary; he found in her a perfect example of God visiting his grace, unearned, upon the most humble." 19 Mary is seen more and more by Christians not as a deity to be worshipped, but as a chosen, favored one. That she forever remained a virgin contradicts the New Testament. As Sweet observes, the question was not whether virginity was a higher form of life than marriage. The ordinance of God would make Joseph and Mary, after their marriage, one. "The marriage relationship is compatible with holy living and Mary is to be considered a human being under the ordinary obligations of human life." 20

All Things Possible

After her visit with Elizabeth, Mary returned to Nazareth. It was here that she had to tell Joseph of the impending birth of Jesus. In all likelihood this would be the most difficult of conversations. Matthew says no more than "this is how Jesus Christ was born. A young woman named Mary was engaged to Joseph from King David's family. But before they were married, she learned that she was going to have a baby by God's Holy Spirit. Joseph was a good man and did not want to embarrass Mary in front of everyone. So he decided to quietly call off the wedding" (Matthew 1:18–19). Mary was in a most precarious position. The scriptures give us no hint of any instructions for Mary. She probably told Joseph her condition after her return from the visit to Elizabeth. She could not hide her pregnancy much longer. She must talk with Joseph, but how would he react?

The punishment for adultery could be severe in those days. Mary was considered to be betrothed, a much stronger word than engaged. Betrayal by the betrothed person could be punished by death. When

Gabriel said that with God all things are possible, He meant more than the conception of Jesus. He meant that God would control all circumstances of the birth of Christ. The angelic joy would have to visit Joseph to validate Mary's story.

Thus Mary's image in the nativity story can be summarized as puzzled and reflective. She was anxious but somehow remained calm. She was also opportunistic in her visit to Elizabeth. She sang a prophetic hymn in praise to her God. Certainly the Holy Spirit guided her path, and the angel Gabriel blessed her with his message. Her life would always be one of high hopes and bitter sorrows. She finally experienced the joy promised her when her Son rose from the dead. Of all women, she was indeed blessed, and her story has resounded through the ages.

The Angels and Joseph, a Series of Dreams

Matthew 1; Luke 2:1–21

Martin Copenhaven wrote an article in the *Journal for Preachers* while he was serving the Wellesley Congregational Church in Wellesley, Massachusetts. The article, "Jesus' Other Parent," expresses Copenhaven's concern that Joseph has often been a background player in the nativity story: "Are there no songs to be sung for him? Visit the world's great cathedrals and look at the stained glass depictions of the nativity, or flip through a book of religious art, and you will see countless renderings of Mary and the babe, beautiful and glowing portraits of the mother and child. Sometimes Joseph isn't even depicted, as if he were nosed out of the scene by the cows and the sheep that press toward the manger, or as if he were cut out of the painting, as one might crop a snapshot. Even when Joseph makes it into the family portrait, he looks more like a bystander than a participant in the scene, as if he is merely part of the scenery rather than a player in the drama." 21

However, in reading Matthew's account of the nativity, we see that

Joseph was a leading figure. He warranted deep concern from the angels. The angels had to bring joy to the man who had and would suffer to understand his favor with God. God chose not only the mother of Jesus; God chose the earthly father. The book of Matthew describes Joseph's predicament this way, "But before they were married, she learned that she was going to have a baby by God's Holy Spirit. Joseph was a good man and did not want to embarrass Mary in front of everyone. So he decided to quietly call off the wedding" (1:18–19). Alfred Plummer summarizes Joseph's reactions when he learned of Mary's pregnancy as "his dismay, and perplexity, his humane decision, and his submission to the Divine decree." That an annunciation to Joseph was necessary was never in doubt. Plummer adds, "He could not have believed so amazing a story, if he had only Mary's word for it." 22

Mary's announcement of her supernatural pregnancy to Joseph must have occurred after her visit to Elizabeth. One can only wonder what and when she finally decided to tell Joseph. C.M. Kerr, a contributor to the *International Standard Bible Encyclopedia*, concurs that Mary must have broken the startling news after her return from Elizabeth's house. Kerr assesses Joseph as a "simple, honest, hard-working, God-fearing man, who was possessed of large sympathies and a warm heart." 23

An angel appeared to Joseph in a dream as he faced the most difficult decision of his life. Joseph was contemplating a quiet divorce. Plummer expresses the difficulty of the situation by reminding that the Jews regarded betrothal as more than an engagement; the betrothal could only be severed by divorce. 24

The book of Matthew emphasizes that Joseph was a good man. Matthew 1:1–16 traces the family lineage of Joseph back to King David and Abraham. Later the book tells the story of Jesus's visit back to Nazareth at the beginning of His ministry. At this time, Jesus was called the carpenter's son, demonstrating that Joseph was well known in the community (Matthew 13:55). Gerald Kleba in his book *Joseph*

Remembered thinks of Joseph as an artisan. He writes, "Craftsmen at that time did not make the ordinary, crude, or simple items that any peasant fancied he could make."25 Joseph was a special man, a good man with an immense decision to make. While this good man was thinking about his possible decisions, an angel revealed the joyful news that Mary's baby would be from the Holy Spirit. This angel told Joseph all of this joyful revelation and advised: "Go ahead and marry her. Then after her baby is born name Him Jesus, because He will save His people from their sins" (Matthew 1:20–21).

Joseph was comforted, assured, and relieved by the words of the angel. How much of God's special favor did he comprehend? He has never been pictured as a reflective soul. He did not "ponder" as Mary did. But his patient and good demeanor must be evidence of a thinking man. After the revelation of the angel, he did not contemplate any more divorcing or abandoning Mary, the woman that he loved. Matthew's account records that they were married (Matthew 1:24). Luke's account only refers to Mary as betrothed (Luke 2:5). Leon Morris offers this opinion of Luke's wording; "Perhaps because, though they were married, the marriage was not yet consummated." 26

Their marriage ceremony must have been out of the ordinary. The scriptures have not given us an account of what took place. Marriage ceremonies of this time usually consisted of a procession in which the bridegroom's friends went by night to bring the bride and her attendants to the home of the groom. The marriage supper would follow, generally in the home of the groom. We can only wonder how the stories of Mary and Joseph affected their family and friends as the scriptures tell us none of the reactions. The people of Nazareth knew the family and acknowledged in later times, as mentioned before, that Jesus was the carpenter's son. Was there a certain amount of stigma attached to the proceedings? How much support from the community did the couple receive? It must be concluded that at this time much of the joy from the angels consisted mainly in Mary and Joseph's faith in God rather than encouragement from family, friends, and neighbors. When the time for the birth came, Matthew 1:23 offers a passage from Isaiah 7:14 to validate the Jewish credentials of the occasion. Alfred Plummer views the genealogy and the Isaiah prophecy as crucial to the entire nativity. The main points which Matthew wished to convey to the reader were the physical reality of the birth of Christ from a virgin and the legality of His descent from David. If Christ had no human parent, He could not have taken on human characteristics. The Messiah was born in the flesh, not of the flesh. He was born in the flesh and therefore was able to vanquish sin and death. Joseph accepted the message of the angel. He was fully persuaded that Mary's condition was that of a virgin. Plummer notes that there was no doubt of this fact.

After the birth of Jesus, Joseph and Mary had marital relations (Matthew 1:25). Plummer refers to the Greek word *eginosken*, which conveys the idea of a sexual relationship. 27 R.T. France in his commentary writes, "The marriage was thus formally completed, but not consummated before the birth of Jesus." France adds, "Therefore Jesus' brothers were subsequently born of Joseph and Mary in the normal way. There is no biblical warrant for the tradition of the perpetual virginity of Mary." 28

The book of Luke sets the rest of the nativity story in the context of secular history. Sometime after the pregnancy was revealed by the angel's message, Joseph was ordered to return to his ancestral home because of a Roman census. The census must not have occurred until the late stages of Mary's pregnancy. Why did he take Mary with him to Bethlehem as the journey would be extremely difficult? Leon Morris conjectures that "perhaps Joseph did not care to leave her at Nazareth. To have remained behind may have exposed her to calumny."29 We can conclude that Mary wished to accompany Joseph, and that he wanted her with him. Did they perceive this census as part of the plan of God? The angels of God had not mentioned this, and in all probability Joseph and

Mary were ignorant of this part of the plan.

At this point another misconception about Joseph must be explored. Joseph has traditionally been seen as much older than Mary. The scriptures have not indicated this nor have they described Joseph as disabled in any way. The journey was difficult, and a strong man was needed to help Mary on her journey. Coupled with the age misconception has been the tradition that Joseph was a widower with children. The scriptures have nowhere mentioned this type of situation. The question would certainly have arisen as to why these alleged children were not mentioned while Joseph was absent on this journey. Kleba in his book places great emphasis on the journey. "There were other people from David's line making the same journey. Still there were dangers from sickness and starvation, brigands and bandits. There were deserts and ridges and miles of desolate land. There was the crippling coldness of camping under the stars and starless nights that were darker than a thousand midnights. Sometimes there was a shortage of water." 30

Luke told the story concisely: "About that time Emperor Augustus gave orders for all the people to be listed in record books. These first records were made when Quirinius was governor of Syria. All had to go to their own hometown to be listed. So Joseph had to leave Nazareth in Galilee and go to Bethlehem in Judea. Long ago Bethlehem had been King David's hometown, and Joseph went there because he was from David's family" (1:1–4). Luke did not mention other children of Joseph traveling with them. He simply wrote, "Mary was engaged to Joseph and traveled with him to Bethlehem. She was soon going to have a baby, and while they were there, she gave birth to her first born son" (1:5–7). The month of Mary's pregnancy was not mentioned nor the length of time that they stayed in Bethlehem after arrival. Certainly, the promise of the angel was in Joseph's mind as they arrived in Bethlehem.

As previously mentioned, the angel had not told Joseph and Mary about this journey. The Roman Empire and its power intervened for a time in the lives of this wonderful couple. Leon Morris writes about the careful—almost obsessive—record keeping of Augustus Caesar. "There is no record of any law of Augustus that a universal census be held. But he did reorganize Roman administration, and there are records of censuses held in a number of places. In Egypt, where the custom is unlikely to have differed significantly from neighboring Syria (of which province Judea was a part), a census was held every fourteen years. When Augustus died he left in his own handwriting a summary of information, such as statistics on direct and indirect taxation, which would not have been derived from censuses. The evidence seems best satisfied if we understand the decree of which Luke writes, not as formal law, but as an administrative direction which set the whole process in motion and has its effect in distant Judea." 31

In her splendid book *Augustus*, Pat Southern writes that Augustus Caesar conducted a census in 8 B.C. and 6 A.D. She notes that Augustus stated that he conducted the census of 8 B.C. with consular power. Southern referred to 8 B. C. as a busy year for Augustus. "He records that he completed another census, where 4,233,000 citizens were registered. Augustus had also carried out censuses in 28 B.C. before he was emperor and 14 A. D., the year of his death, with the help of Tiberius." 32 Southern acknowledges that Augustus conducted censuses with regularity. These were used for tax purposes as well as a record of the population.

The date of the census of Joseph and his family would have started in Rome in 8 B. C. and arrived in Judea years later. Most scholars have placed the birth of Jesus as 7 to 5 B. C. Thus Joseph would have been obeying Roman law as well as the law of the province of Syria that controlled Judea. Also, Augustus' successor, Tiberius, conducted censuses that were for tax purposes throughout the lifetime of Jesus. In her biography *Tiberius the Politician*, Barbara Levick mentions a particular date of 34 A.D. in which Judea and Syria as well as Achaea in Greece were at the point of revolt because of high taxation following a census.33

Joseph had received the message of joy from the angel, but the message was complex. The message to wed Mary was not an easy choice. Their family would doubtless incur gossip and disbelief. Even with almost identical testimonies coming from the wedded couple, their road would be difficult. The census taking in Bethlehem made matters even more difficult for them. The book of Luke continues to tell the birth story in simple terms. They found no place to lodge (2:7). Morris conjectures that Joseph may have left too late on his journey. The innkeeper may not have wanted them because of Mary's condition. It may have been a long and difficult journey and their reservations cancelled. 34 The facts were there, but Luke's account does not give us the answer. Still, Joseph remembered the words of assurance from the angel.

The Angels and the Shepherds

Luke 2:1–21

In Luke's Gospel, as mentioned, the birth of Jesus is described in very simple terms. The baby Jesus was resting in a manger or feeding trough for animals. The place of birth has been conjectured to be a stable or an attached dwelling where animals were kept. Some traditions have obtained support that the birth of Jesus took place in one of the caves in the region of Bethlehem. I, myself, was once taken to such a cave, and it would have been quite accommodating for many people. But, as Leon Morris has aptly admitted, "We do not know. We know that everything points to poverty, obscurity, and rejection. That Mary wrapped the child herself points to a lonely birth."35

The family of Jesus must have needed further assurance at this critical time, and God provided. God sent His angels not to kings or other ruling officials, but to shepherds. The choice of shepherds has always intrigued scholars. Shepherds did not have the best of reputations and were considered unclean and unreliable. These shepherds mentioned by Luke were keeping flocks in the area of Bethlehem, and the sheep were in all probability destined for priestly sacrifice.

It was also appropriate that, as the birth was in Bethlehem, the home of the shepherd king, David, shepherds would be part of the story. These shepherds were chosen by God to be the first visitors to see Jesus. The announcement of the birth came in spectacular fashion: "the splendor of the Lord shone around them" (Luke 2:9). An angel brought words of joy to the shepherds: "'Don't be afraid! I have good news for you, which will make everyone happy. This very day in King David's hometown a Savior was born for you. He is Christ the Lord. You will know who he is, because you will find him dressed in baby clothes and lying on a bed of hay.' Suddenly many other angels came down from heaven and joined in praising God. They said, 'Praise God in heavens! Peace on earth to everyone who pleases God'" (Luke 2:10–14).

The emphasis of the angel's words was on the joy that the birth of Jesus would bring. Just as Gabriel had spoken to Mary of the favor that God had shown her, and as the angel had brought consolation and joy to Joseph, this angel spoke to common men to whom Jesus would bring joy through His saving grace. God chose shepherds to hear His glorious message because they were of humble origin. Though they weren't always respected, they were given the incredible opportunity in this case to make the first visit to see Jesus. Jesus would be found by them for He would be the only baby born at that time in such humble circumstances in a stable. What did the shepherds bring to their savior? They had nothing to bring but themselves. God chose to make this first announcement of birth to rough-clothed men who made their living in the fields.

As Joseph and Mary were making the baby as comfortable as possible, these shepherds arrived. What did these parents think? In the film, *The Nativity Story*, there is a scene during the long trek to Bethlehem where Joseph wondered how he would be able to teach Jesus.36 Now he was even more surprised to see shepherds entering the stable area. The shepherds must have told the parents of the angelic revelation, and how this child would one day bring peace to earth among those that God favored.

The parents and any others who were present were amazed at the story that the shepherds told. These simple, working men had experienced a unique encounter with the angels of God. The shepherds were filled with praise to God because of the joyous news that they heard from the angels. Of the two parents, Mary is described in Luke as the reflective one. She pondered the events that took place. Leon Morris observes that she "treasured all this, and retained it in the innermost recesses of her being."[37] The appearance of the angel Gabriel had begun her bouts of deep thought. After visiting the shepherds, these angels returned to the heavenly realms, having completed another mission.

Jesus would later call Himself the Good Shepherd (John 10:11,14). Perhaps He had heard the story from Joseph and Mary about his first Bethlehem visitors. The good shepherds protect and care for their sheep. The angels of the nativity had found good shepherds in their visit to Bethlehem.

The Angels and Joseph, Other Dreams

Matthew 2

Gerald Kleba describes Joseph as the silent dreamer. Just as his namesake in the Old Testament, this Joseph would dream many dreams, and angels would comfort and protect him. His experiences regarding the wedding with Mary and the subsequent birth of Jesus in Bethlehem had been very overwhelming. How far his life had changed from the mundane world of the carpenter and craftsman that he had been cannot be estimated. Now he was the earthly father of the Messiah. Kleba reckons that Joseph, Mary, and the shepherds shared their stories of the angelic appearances together.

The scriptures do not tell us of the immediate days following the birth, but the rite of circumcision for the baby Jesus would take place on the eighth day and would be administered by the local mohel. 38 The rite of circumcision was most important in Jewish society. Morris comments, "Jesus was circumcised on the eighth day in accordance with Jewish law (Genesis 17:12). He was born under the law, to redeem those who were under the law (Galatians 4:4) and was then subjected to the requirements of the law. Emphasis is on the name of the child with the name given by the angel. The divine purpose is to be seen in the name." 39

At this point in time another visit must be examined. According to Matthew's Gospel Jesus and His family received a second set of visitors while Jesus was still an infant. A scholarly consensus has placed this visit after the visit of the shepherds. By the time of the visit of the magi or wise men, living arrangements had changed. Following a super star or nova, the magi are lead to and enter a house (*oikos*), a different word than was used by Luke as the site of the birth of Jesus (Matthew 2:11). The visit of the magi most likely occurred months after the birth, and Jesus would have long since finished His presentation at the temple and been witnessed and blessed by the prophets Simeon and Anna (Luke 2:22–40). The family of Jesus was thus living in a home, in all likelihood rented. *The Life Application Bible Commentary* has found one solution for the timeline of events. "Jesus was probably one or two years old (a young child) when the wise men found him. By this time, Mary and Joseph were married, living in a house and intending to stay in Bethlehem for a while."40 The venerable scholar J. W. McGarvey reinforces this belief when he writes, "Joseph intended to make Bethlehem his home in the future." 41

The magi themselves were an interesting group, dramatically opposite on the social ladder as the shepherds. R.T. France in his study of Matthew's Gospel explains the magi in this way: "The wise men are more correctly Magi, originally the name of a Persian priestly caste, but later used widely for magicians and astrologers, a numerous class in most countries in Western Asia at the time. Astrology had been developed into a sophisticated science especially in Babylon, and there is evidence for its influence also in Palestine. From what part of the East these Magi came can only be guessed; their gifts are most likely of Arabian origin, but would be available to and used by the Magi of Babylonia, and this is perhaps their most likely place of origin." 42

During this period of time Joseph had assumed his role as protector of the home. He had made a decision to rent or own a house in Bethlehem. In so doing he had taken on the parental duties of Jesus's earthly father. One might assume that during the family's stay in Bethlehem, Joseph returned to his profession as carpenter and craftsman. As stated, the natives of Nazareth would later call Jesus the carpenter's son. Joseph had obeyed the message of the angel who had told him in a dream to take Mary as his bride and to name her baby Jesus. And he had seen the promise come true as Matthew recorded: "Just as the prophet had said, a virgin will have a baby boy, and he will be called Immanuel, which means God is with us" (Matthew 1:23).

The gifts of the magi, which consisted of gold, frankincense, and myrrh, must have overwhelmed Joseph. He certainly could not afford such gifts. He must have marveled at the length of their journey to see Jesus. Plummer observes that there "is abundant evidence of a wide-spread desire and expectation of a coming Deliverer or universal King some time before the Birth of Christ." Certainly there were planetary conjunctions during this time period, but whether these attracted the attention of the magi cannot be determined. It was certainly ironic that pagans were so enthralled with certain signs that were revealed to them through astrological clues that they were willing to make such a long and arduous journey. Yet, the Jewish hierarchy with Pentateuch and prophetic writings in hand were far from being elated from this news and did not bother to verify such until forced by King Herod. 43

The magi and their visit are well documented in Matthew. Matthew's Jewish background did not prevent him from acknowledging the scope of this joyous birth. Matthew did not present history just to suit his own ethnic agenda. Therefore, as Joseph examined these precious gifts from the magi, he might have at first thought of their material value. The gift of gold, most likely in the form of Roman gold coins, would have been worth a fortune. Frankincense and myrrh were religious in connotation and even priestly in function. Joseph and Mary could quickly see both the regal riches bestowed on Jesus as well as the highest form of religious homage. Joseph now was certain that the message of the angel had been verified. The child Jesus was indeed *Immanuel*, God with us. The magi who followed that super star or nova increased the faith and assurance of this chosen family.

The story of the magi has always been connected with Herod, the Judean king. Herod was intensely concerned about his own position as king. As R. T. France mentions, "Herod's concern is understandable: as an Edomite and a Roman appointee, he was vulnerable to the claims of a king of the true Davidic dynasty. His later years were plagued by the fear of rivals."44 McGarvey explains Herod's reaction to the request of the magi's search for the King of the Jews. The trouble of Herod, when he heard the inquiry of the strangers, was natural: "Being near the close of his own reign, and naturally anxious concerning the succession to the throne, he could not hear with equanimity that the founder of a rival dynasty had been born. All Jerusalem was troubled with him because they dreaded a conflict between two claimants for the throne." 45 Many historians have concluded that Herod was not a rightful heir to the throne of David since he was descended from Esau. He was an Idumean Arab but considered himself Jewish by religion.46

Much of the Jewish population despised Herod as a usurper. Herod himself ruled by force and thought that some type of revolution would overthrow his rule. Herod realized many Jews were expecting a Messiah who would be a great military and political leader. Herod, because of these suspicions, called together all of the chief priests and scribes. He wanted the expert opinion that they could provide as to where Jesus would be born. These experts provided a passage in the Old Testament from the prophet Micah, the fifth chapter and the second verse. "And thou Bethlehem in the land of Judah, are not the least among the princes of Judah: for out of thee shall come a Governor that shall rule my people Israel." Another translation of Micah states, " But you, Bethlehem, in the land of Judah, are by no means least among the rulers of Judah; for out of you will come a ruler who will be the shepherd of my people Israel."

Peter Richardson in his biography of Herod identifies Herod as being just as interested in the Roman and Hellenistic world as he was in Jewish culture. "From his father and grandfather Herod inherited a generous measure of interest in the Hellenistic world, a fondness for things Roman, an acute sense of political opportunity, and perhaps an autocratic style." 47 Herod, later called the Great—not because of his moral fiber but rather his firm political savvy and vast building programs—became a powerful player in the politics of the Roman Empire. He was responsible for the construction of cities such as Caesarea Maritima, Herodium, and Masada and for the temple in Jerusalem that would bear his name. But now he was concerned with succession. He had even executed some of his family to prevent the semblance of rebellion. Now, Herod planned to use these magi from the East along with the expertise of his Jewish scholars to eradicate this probable new Messiah. McGarvey concludes that Herod already had a plan for his soldiers to kill the Messiah. Herod was looking for exact information. He could deduce from the time of the nova star's appearance the child's age. If the nova star appeared a couple of years earlier then he would murder all male children under the age of two. 48

Thankfully, the diabolical schemes of Herod did not disturb the joyous occasion of the magi's visit. After the completion of their visit, the Lord warned them in a dream of Herod's intentions. Then the magi returned to their homes by a different route and avoided Herod. Sometime, perhaps in a matter of days, an angel appeared to Joseph in a dream. This dream was definitely a warning. Joseph was instructed to leave Judea for Egypt where Herod would have no power to harm Joseph's family. And thus the joy of Jesus' birth was protected by *Yahweh*, the Heavenly Father. Joseph, just as he had reacted when he heard the message to wed Mary, obeyed the message and acted immediately. The journey would be difficult, and he must have remembered a similar difficult journey to Bethlehem.

The length of time that Joseph and Mary spent in Egypt has not been disclosed in scripture. The location of the residence in Egypt is not mentioned. However, this period of time must have been one of reflection for the family. Perhaps Joseph and Mary thought at great lengths how they would teach this child. Although Joseph has left us no record of his thoughts through his speaking, his actions were always obedient to the word of *Yahweh* and the voice of the angels.

Herod Examined

In the meantime Herod realized that the magi had deceived him. The paranoia of this powerful king was exhibited in his later years. As he had executed family members including sons and at least one wife, he would now attempt to destroy the male infants of Bethlehem. The actual number of casualties has never been completely determined. R.T. France estimates the number as not more than twenty as Bethlehem was but a small village at that time. He further states that "perhaps Matthew intends us to see also in Bethlehem's mourning a temporary sorrow, out of which God will bring joy and deliverance through Bethlehem's Messiah, returning from a foreign land; there is no precise correspondence, but the relevance lies in the perception of God's working through disaster to blessing, through death to life." 49

When Herod died in 4 B.C., he left a very complex legacy. The Bible historian Henry Dosker in an article in the *International Standard Bible Encyclopedia* relates that Herod died "unmourned and unbeloved by his own people to pass into history as a name soiled by violence and blood." He compares Herod to Nero in his domestic relationships. Herod executed his wife, Marianne, and his sons: Alexander, Aristobulus, and Antipater. Even the Emperor Augustus was wary of Herod's violent behavior. The emperor was quoted in 7 B.C. as saying that "he would rather be Herod's hog than his son." Augustus knew that Herod would follow Jewish dietary laws, and that a hog would be safer around Herod than a possible heir. The Herodian lineage continued to persecute Jesus and John the Baptist. Dosker concludes, "History tells us of few more immoral families than the house of Herod, which by intermarriage of its members so entangled the genealogical tree as to make it a veritable puzzle. As these marriages were nearly all within the line of forbidden consanguinity, under the Jewish law, they still further embittered the people of Israel against the Herodian family." 50

William M. Willett in his classic biography of Herod remarks that Herod's family was one of the wealthiest in Jerusalem. Upon his death his wealth had multiplied as evidenced by his numerous palaces. These assets would later be distributed among his surviving children.51

Peter Richardson observes that the conditions of wealth and succession intermingled in Herod's mind along with the prevailing Messianic expectations of this period. In reference to New Testament accounts of Herod's reign, Richardson suggests the following: "Both John the Baptist and Jesus were born late in Herod's reign; the birth of Jesus may have been in 7B.C., two-and-a-half years before Herod's death; the tradition of the massacre of the innocents reflected Herod's succession problems and the execution of three of his own children; the flight to Egypt derived from scriptural allusions that were plausible because of the difficult conditions at the end of Herod's reign." 52

Herod sought to enshrine himself in history by mentioning his accomplishments. These have been found on original bronze tablets residing in Caesarea Maratima and contain a list of twenty-eight items. Some of these tablets state, "I improved social justice with new laws encouraging support of Torah. I suppressed discussion among the people and even in my own family, and I put an end to revolutionaries who tyrannized the common people. In addition to the Temple in Jerusalem, may the Lord be praised, I showed my piety in a memorial to the Patriarchs and Matriarchs in Hebron, another to Abraham at Mamreh, one to King David in Jerusalem, and in tombs for my own family. I built temples to Roma and Augustus in Caesarea, Sebaste, and Panias, reconstructed a temple in Rhodes, and helped complete a temple in Si'a. At the time of writing I am in the seventieth year of my age and will soon be gathered to my fathers. My body is to be laid in Herodian, my mausoleum and favorite retreat. May Judea long be blessed under Rome's beneficent oversight and the rule of my children and children's children. Dated at Jericho, in the consulship of C. Calvisius Sabenus and L. Pasienus Rufus, year one of the 193rd Olympiad and year 37 of my reign."[53]

Joseph and Another Angel Decree

Matthew 2:19–23

Herod's assessment of his life was one of earthly accomplishments. His personal life was much more unflattering. At the time of his death, another angel was sent to Joseph. Matthew related the return of Joseph and his family to Nazareth. The message of this angel was protective in nature. Again in a dream, the angel said, "Get up, take the child and his mother and go to the land of Israel, for those who were trying to take the child's life are dead" (Matthew 2:20).

Jesus was now referred to as a child, not a baby, indicating some passage of time. This message to Joseph must have comforted him. Although Joseph's family must have found help in Egypt among the various colonies of Jews who lived there, and thus protection from Herod, a longing for the homeland remained. The book of Matthew also shows the completion of prophecy when recording Hosea's words, "Out of Egypt I have called my son" (Hosea 11:1; Matthew 2:15). Many citations from the Old Testament could be referenced including Moses and, of course, Joseph, the son of Jacob.

When the angel spoke to Joseph, the messages of protection were completed. Joseph must have chosen Judea at first to avoid criticisms from the people of Nazareth, but when he heard that Herod Archelaus had succeeded his father, he decided that Nazareth would be safer. This return to Israel certainly demonstrates Joseph's concern for the complete protection of his family. God had indeed chosen the best earthly father available. Matthew also saw another Old Testament prophecy fulfilled when he wrote, "He will be called a Nazarene" (Matthew 2:23). R.T. France interprets the various prophecies in this manner: "The word prophet suggests that it is not meant to be a quotation of a specific passage, but a summary of a theme of prophetic explanation. Thus it has been suggested that Matthew saw in the obscurity of Nazareth the fulfillment of Old Testament indications of a humble and rejected Messiah; for Jesus to be known by the derogatory epithet, *Nazoraios* was not compatible with the expected royal dignity of the Messiah."54

The family made another long journey. This time the journey was from Egypt to Galilee. The journey must have been less stressful than the rushed escape from Bethlehem to flee the wrath of Herod. The boy Jesus was now older, perhaps several years older. As mentioned, most scholars have placed the birth of Jesus from around five to seven years B.C. This would put His age at about two when the trip to Nazareth was made.

The family did have to avoid Herod Archelaus. It has been concluded from history that he was no better morally than his father and was deposed by his own people for misrule in 6 A.D. 55

Angels—The Nativity and Beyond

The messages of the angels of the nativity end here. These messages brought joy and celebration, warning, and finally comfort and protection. Jesus was now ready to begin his years in Nazareth. Later in his book, Luke records a journey Jesus made to Jerusalem when He was twelve years of age. His unique and divine mission was already making itself known to not only His parents but to those who heard Him (Luke 2:41–52). In Egypt God had kept His Son safe as He had protected Israel in ancient times. Out of Egypt God called His Son to liberate mankind as He had liberated Israel many years before. The Messianic prophecy that began in the Old Testament would foretell the ultimate Messianic story of Jesus. 56

The examples of messages from the angels continue throughout the New Testament. But before looking at these examples, a great compliment must be paid to Joseph as has already been paid to Mary. McGarvey mentions Joseph's intention on making Bethlehem the family hone. The evil intentions of Herod and his son Herod Archelaus prevented this. In every case Joseph followed the instructions of God as they were made known to him. As McGarvey comments, "His prompt compliance with all these heavenly directions, and this in behalf of a child that was not his own, shows how fit a man he was for the momentous trust committed to his hands." 57

The angels of the nativity appeared in sequences to spread the message of God to Zechariah, Mary, the shepherds, and finally to the earthly father of Jesus. The messages pursued themes of joy, warning, and comfort. Similar messages continued to God's people in the New Testament. Angels assisted Christians like Stephen at the time of his martyrdom and Peter when he was in prison. The New Testament emphasizes angelic concern for Christians throughout the first century.

Angels did indeed assist God's people throughout the New Testament. But what happened to those select few who received angelic messages during the nativity? The shepherds are never mentioned again except that they became symbolic of the everyday people hearing the teachings of Jesus. In Luke 4:18–19, Jesus quoted from the prophet Isaiah when he told the members of the synagogue that He came to bring joy to the poor. The shepherds were part of those who would have been considered poor.

Zechariah and Joseph—After the Nativity

Zechariah the priest is not mentioned after the birth of John the Baptist. Luke described John's parents as old when John was born. Did they live to witness his ministry as a forerunner of Jesus? Perhaps this would have been unlikely, and John has been pictured as a solitary individual. Whatever the case, Zechariah and Elizabeth are not mentioned again even at the time of John's martyrdom. John's disciples carried out the burial arrangements.

Joseph, the earthly father of Jesus, is mentioned in a personal way in Luke 2:41–42. When Jesus accompanied His parents to the Passover Feast, Joseph was seen as a religious man observing Jewish law. He had always been of this persuasion as he followed the rites of circumcision, dedication, and purification. Joseph was serving as a good role model to Jesus on the journey to the Passover Feast as Jesus was now considered no longer an infant but a *pais* or boy. Leon Morris believes that there was some significance to the age of twelve as "it was at thirteen years of age that a Jewish boy could become a son of the commandment or full member of the synagogue. He would then assume all the responsibilities implied in his circumcision."58

As Joseph and Mary journeyed back from Jerusalem to Nazareth, the feast being completed, they discovered that they had lost Jesus. After what must have been a period of intense searching, including a return to Jerusalem, they found him among the teachers in the temple. The teachers of the Mosaic Law were amazed at the understanding of this twelve year old. In another way Joseph and Mary were astonished (Luke 43–47). Morris thinks, "Jesus had a relationship to God shared by no other. Joseph and Mary did not understand this." 59 Joseph must have remembered the angel's protection of the baby Jesus, and now was witnessing the maturity of Jesus as He discussed the Jewish law.

As noted, Joseph was mentioned at a later time during Jesus' ministry. Joseph was the carpenter as Jesus was called the carpenter's son. Since he is not included in the New Testament with Mary and her sons in following Jesus, Joseph seems to be no longer active. However, an early death is not stated in the scriptures, and he must have indeed had occasion to at least teach Jesus a customary trade according to Jewish tradition. Luke 2:52 mentions that Jesus grew in wisdom and stature and in favor with God and man. As mentioned, Joseph, as his earthly father, was not verbally described as reflective, but his actions revealed understanding and obedience. He was certainly described as sensitive and caring toward Mary. He was very careful to keep the Mosaic Law. He most likely supervised Jesus in educational values such as synagogue school. He shared Mary's concern for the safety of Jesus and was amazed with her at the actions of Jesus. He fulfilled a unique position in a most admirable way. Conjecture about his life beyond the Passover journey cannot be verified. The time of his death has remained a mystery, but he always followed the words of the angels when they spoke to him.

Mary Experiences the Fulfillment of the Angel Message

The last person to be described will always be the best known to have received the nativity message of an angel. Mary's life has been recorded in scripture from the appearance of Gabriel until the time of her fellowship with Christian believers found in Luke's writings in the Book of Acts. Most estimates of her age would place her at fifty or more by the time the Acts reference was documented. Mary, of all the chosen to receive the nativity message of the angels, has been honored the most.

The scriptures describe her as a pensive woman. She must have been uneducated in a formal setting, but naturally gifted in recognizing the special qualities of her Son. As her husband Joseph, she was obedient to the angelic message. As Jesus becamc older, and specifically when He was apparently lost in Jerusalem, Mary demonstrated concern and agitation. As a mother she would be proud of her son's intellectual and spiritual progress, but she was angry at His apparent neglect of parental authority (Luke 2:48). Parents have always wanted to know the location of their children.

Mary was no different and, if anything, was even more concerned after receiving Gabriel's message about the special nature of this child. She was not afraid to make those concerns known to her Son. Even after contemplating Messianic beliefs about Jesus, she could not understand the ways of Jesus which were so unusual and unexpected. She must have pondered from the very beginning to the advent of the Christian church the meanings of many experiences. Louis Sweet realizes her story could not have been fabricated, and her life was always touched with even unconscious traits of truth.60 Compared to the other lives these angels touched, she seemed to study their message the most thoroughly.

John's Gospel records her first encounter with the adult Jesus at the wedding feast in Cana. Twenty years passed since Mary questioned her Son and criticized Him for leaving the safety of His parents (Luke 2:48). She had not comprehended His love for the teachings of the Law at such an early age. Yet she remained aware of His unusual powers. In the second chapter of John's Gospel, a wedding feast in the village of Cana was taking place. Mary was the first to believe her Son had extraordinary power. Her appeal to Jesus did not result in disappointment and, as Sweet observes, as Jesus followed her request, His glory was manifested. 61

The story of the miracle at Cana is recorded in John's Gospel with simplicity. "There was a marriage in Cana of Galilee, and the mother of Jesus was there" (John 2:1). The distinguished writer B. F. Westcott believes that Mary was closely connected with the wedding party and was at the wedding festivities well before Jesus arrived. Westcott thinks that the lack of mention of Joseph at the occasion and at later events implied that he had passed away.62

On this occasion Mary must have thought the opportunity was a great time for Jesus to demonstrate His power. She remembered the visit of Gabriel and the angelic promises that had been fortified by the visits of the shepherds and the magi (Luke 2:8–21; Matthew 2:1–12). Prophecies by Simeon and Anna (Luke 2:22–39) helped her see the special nature of her

Son. The escape from Bethlehem and the return to Nazareth (Matthew 2:13–23) made her envision a great destiny for Jesus. At some point she assumed that Jesus would demonstrate His power from God.

When she asked Jesus for help at this occasion, Westcott observes that Jesus pondered about the time and the place. He was not dependent on suggestions even though the suggestions came from His mother.63 Mary had the intuition to believe that Jesus would make things right, and very likely she remembered the details with John the Apostle concerning the happy outcome. Westcott summarizes, "We cannot but conclude from the minuteness of the details of the history that the Mother of the Lord made known some of them to the apostle to whose care she was entrusted. Moreover in this miracle only does she occupy a prominent place."64

Mary certainly heeded the message of Gabriel in regard to watching out for the wellbeing of her Son even when He was an adult. The book of Mark records an incident when Mary and the brothers of Jesus attempted to force Him into a period of retirement from His ministry (Mark 3:20–35). Sweet thinks of it as "retirement for a time," encouraged by "loving anxiety." 65 Without a doubt the family, even Mary, were still unclear of the mission of Jesus at this time. Accusations by various religious leaders that Jesus was possessed of demons surely were heard by Mary. Though confused, Mary still knew that He had special powers from God. At this point the question has often been posed as to the belief of the brothers and sisters of Jesus. Were they attempting to protect a family member whom they thought was mentally unbalanced? Mark 6:3 mentions the four brothers by name. Luke 4:14–21 does not mention their presence at the synagogue in Nazareth when Jesus announced His mission. John 7:5 states that the brothers were not believers.

A conclusion can be made that during much of His ministry the earthly family was unsure of His mission. Even Mary could not fully comprehend the events that would happen. Simeon's prophecy that

Mary's soul would be pierced with a sword would take place. Mary had heard Jesus explain that His true relatives were in the kingdom of heaven. Mary would require the entire ministry of her Son to know He was indeed the promised Messiah. Mary was present at the crucifixion of Her Son. Mark 15:40 says that the women at the cross were Mary Magdalene, Mary (the mother of Jesus), and Salome (the mother of James and John. Mary Magdalene was from Magdala, a town near Capernaum, in the region of the Sea of Galilee. She had been released from demon possession by Jesus. These women had been faithful servants of Jesus, following Him and providing for His material needs.

Yet, these women could do little at the crucifixion. They could not speak before the Sanhedrin for the defense of Jesus. They could not appeal to the Roman Procurator, Pontius Pilate. They could not stop the angry mob or overpower the Roman guards. But they stayed at the cross when almost all of the disciples were absent. Mary is described in John 19:25 as being with the other women at the cross. Jesus entrusted the care of His mother to John, perhaps, in the view of Westcott, as he was closest to a blood relationship to Jesus being the son of the sister of the Lord's mother. 66 The sadness of the scene of crucifixion resonated with John. Mary's hopes that had been promised by the angel were apparently vanished. She felt the full piercing of the sword predicted by Simeon the Prophet. Would angels appear again?

The Gospel writers have unanimously agreed that women came to the tomb of Jesus Christ to assist in the anointing of His body. The tomb had been given to the family of Jesus for burial by Joseph of Arimathea, a prominent Jewish leader who had been influenced by the teachings of Jesus (Luke 23:50). Mary Magdalene and others with the name Mary were mentioned at the tomb. Luke 23:55 mentions a plurality of women at the tomb and concludes that several women lingered by the tomb in a state of uncertainty. The Greek word *loipos* used by Luke can mean simply the remaining or the rest of the group. The Gospel writers emphasized

Mary Magdalene, especially John the Apostle. But it certainly would be conceivable that Jesus' mother would be in that group called the remaining, or the rest. At some point angels, Luke 24:4 mentions two, appeared to the women. They told the women to tell the disciples of the resurrection. Mary, the mother of Jesus, had great opportunity to witness the angelic message.

After the resurrection of Jesus Christ, we have but one other mention of Mary in the New Testament. She was numbered among the believers in the Book of Acts. In Acts 1:14 we can assume that other family members were present. Paul in I Corinthians 15:7 listed James, the brother of Jesus, as having seen the resurrected Christ. Mary, although in the primary care of John the Apostle, must have been thrilled to witness her earthly family as part of the believers. From all indications Mary lived the rest of her life with John the Apostle as her chief caretaker. Evidently the arrangement was congenial to her immediate family. As Sweet observes, " It is also clear that Mary herself and the family, who seemed to be very completely under her influence, whatever may have been their earlier misgivings, never broke with the circle of disciples, and persistently kept within the range of experiences which led at last to full-orbed Christian faith." 67 It was most appropriate that Mary was pictured among believers and in prayer (Acts 1:14). F.F. Bruce says it well when he writes, "This is the last recorded appearance of the Mother of our Lord. It is significant that she is found in prayer with His disciples." 68

Mary had come full circle. The angel's message prophesied her favor with God and the birth of her Son. She lived to either see or hear of the angels' appearance to the women at the tomb. When she first appeared as a young virgin, she praised her God. R.B. Rackham comments that, as she prays with the believers in the Book of Acts, her dominant element in the prayer was praise. 69 The messages of the angels had been successful.

Concluding Thoughts

The Apostle Paul observed that "when the time was right, God sent His Son into the world" (Galatians 4:4). Many older translations speak of the "fullness of time." The classic work by H.E. Dana, *The New Testament World*, summarizes the various historical elements that harmonized at the time of Christ's appearance. Greek culture had permeated the Roman Empire even to the language of the people. Dana writes that Paul used *koine* or the common Greek rather than Latin to compose his epistle to the Roman church. Dana also mentions the effect of a Roman government that formed a great geographical and political union ruled by an Emperor from Rome but allowed to remain diverse in customs and religion. Dana finally mentions the Eastern influence, in particular religion and more specifically the Hebrew traditions. The world in which the angels of the nativity appeared was Jewish: "Jesus was a Jew, Paul was a Jew, all of the first Christians were Jews. Doctrine, practice psychology, and experience in first century Christianity were predominantly Jewish, though advancing constantly in the Hellenistic direction. One therefore cannot begin to study the New Testament without the consideration of the Jewish background. There is repeated reference of various sects, institutions, and customs which originated in preceding centuries of Jewish history, such as the Pharisees, the Saducees, the Sanhedin, the synagogue, and so forth. Well established and familiar modes of expression were used by Jesus such as aphoristic utterances, didactic discourse and parables. Current religious conceptions of standard Judaism are adopted or presupposed by the New Testament, such as God, revelation, immortality, judgment, angels, Messiah, and so forth. The prevailing conditions of Palestinian life are in the background of every verse of the Gospels. These and many other features require knowledge of Jewish life and history for adequate interpretation." 70

God used the angels of the nativity to introduce His Son into the world at the right time, and the angels successfully completed their mission. The writer of Hebrews, as previously mentioned, referenced angels many times. Angels were described as ministering servants who were not to be worshipped. Angels also appeared in the apocalyptic books of the New Testament as triumphant servants, guardians of believers, and the final messengers of the *parousia* or return of Jesus Christ.

While angels have been historically important in the New Testament, their messages began with simple people at the nativity. These messages were filled with hope, comfort, and praise to God. Their messages affected a country priest, lowly shepherds of Bethlehem, a Galilean carpenter, and a maiden from Nazareth. Their messages changed the lives of these simple folk forever. The angels' promises were not always clear to the listeners, but all saw some sort of fulfillment. Mary, who had the greatest burden, saw the complete fruition. She not only experienced the birth but the resurrection of her Son. Her later years were spent in the *koinonia* or community of believers. She even witnessed her own family become leaders of that community. The angels of the nativity must have rejoiced greatly.

Notes

1. John M. Wilson, "Angels," *International Standard Bible Encyclopedia*, Grand Rapids, Michigan, WM. B. Eerdmans Publishing Co., 1960

2. Ibid

3. Carl Braaten, *The Last Things: Biblical and Theological Perspectives on Eschatology*, Grand Rapids, Michigan, WM. B. Eerdmans Publishing Co., 2002

4. Mike Aquilina, *Angels of God*, Cincinnati, St. Anthony Messenger Press, 2009

5. Herbert Lockyer, *All the Angels in the Bible*, Peabody, Massachusetts, Hendrickson Publishers, Inc., 2007

6. Billy Graham, *Angels*, Nashville, Thomas Nelson, 2011

7. Leon Morris, *Luke, Tyndale New Testament Commentaries,* Grand Rapids, Michigan, Inter-Varsity Press, WM. B. Eerdmans Publishing Co., 1999

8. Ibid

9. A.B. Bruce, *The Expositor's Greek Testament*, Grand Rapids, Michigan, WM.B. Eerdmans Publishing Co., 1956

10. Leon Morris, *Luke, Tyndale New Testament Commentaries*, Grand Rapids, Michigan, Inter-Varsity Press, WM. B. Eerdmans Publishing Co. 1999

11. Ibid

12. Louis Sweet, "Mary," *International Standard Bible Encyclopedia*, Grand Rapids, Michigan, WM. B. Eerdmans Publishing Co.,1960

13. Leon Morris, *Luke, Tyndale New Testament Commentaries*, Grand

Rapids, Michigan Inter-Varsity Press, WM. B. Eerdmans Co., 1999

14. Ibid

15. Alfred Plummer, *An Exegetical Commentary on the Gospel According to S. Matthew*, Grand Rapids, Michigan, WM. B. Eerdmans Publishing Co., 1956

16. Leon Morris, *Luke, Tyndale New Testament Commentaries*, Grand Rapids, Michigan, Inter-Varsity Press, WM. B. Eerdmans Publishing Co., 1999

17. Louis Sweet, "Mary," *International Standard Bible Encyclopedia*, Grand Rapids, Michigan, WM. B. Eerdmans Publishing Co., 1960

18. Ibid

19. David Van Biema, "Hail Mary," *Time Magazine*, New York, March 21, 2005

20. Louis Sweet, "Mary," *International Standard Bible Encyclopedia*, Grand Rapids, Michigan, WM. B. Eerdmans Publishing Co., 1960

21. Martin Copenhaven, " Jesus' Other Parent," Montreat, North Carolina, Journal for Preachers

22. Alfred Plummer, *An Exegetical Commentary on the Gospel According to S. Matthew*, Grand Rapids, Michigan, WM. B. Eerdmans Publishing Co., 1956

23. C.M. Kerr, "Joseph," *International Standard Bible Encyclopedia*, Grand Rapids, Michigan, WM. B. Eerdmans Publishing Co., 1960

24. Alfred Plummer, *An Exegetical Commentary on the Gospel According to S. Matthew*, Grand Rapids, Michigan, WM. B. Eerdmans Publishing Co., 1956

25. Gerald Kleba, *Joseph Remembered*, Wyomissing, Pa., Summit

Publishing Co. 2000

26. Leon Morris, *Luke, Tyndale New Testament Commentaries*, Grand Rapids, Michigan, Inter-Varsity Press, WM. B. Eerdmans Publishing Co., 1999

27. Alfred Plummer, *An Exegetical Commentary on the Gospel According to S. Matthew*, Grand Rapids, Michigan, WM. B. Eerdmans Publishing Co., 1956

28. R.T. France, *The Gospel of Matthew*, Grand Rapids, Michigan, WM. B. Eerdmans Publishing Co., 2007

29. Leon Morris, *Luke, Tyndale New Testament Commentaries*, Grand Rapids, Michigan, Inter-Varsity Press, WM. B. Eerdmans Publishing Co., 1999

30. Gerald Kleba, *Joseph Remembered*, Wyomissing, Pa., Summit Publishing Co. 2000

31. Leon Morris, *Luke, Tyndale New Testament Commentaries*, Grand Rapids, Michigan, Inter-Varsity Press, WM. B. Eerdmans Publishing Co., 1999

32. Pat Southern, *Augustus*, London, Routledge, 1999

33. Barbara Levick, *Tiberius the Politician*, London, Routledge, 1999A

34. Leon Morris, *Luke, Tyndale New Testament Commentaries*, Grand Rapids, Michigan, Inter-Varsity Press, WM. B. Eerdmans Publishing Co. 1999

35. Ibid

36. *The Nativity Story*, Cinecitta Studios, Rome, Metropolitan Films France,2006

37. Leon Morris, *Luke, Tyndale New Testament Commentaries*, Grand Rapids, Michigan, Inter-Varsity Press, WM. B. Eerdmans

Publishing Co.,1999

38. Gerald Kleba, *Joseph Remembered*, Wyomissing, Pa., Summit Publishing Company, 2000

39. Leon Morris, *Luke, Tyndale New Testament Commentaries*, Grand Rapids, Michigan, Inter-Varsity Press, WM. B. Eerdmans Publishing Co., 1999

40. *The Life Application Bible Commentary*, Carol Stream, Illinois, Tyndale House Publishers, 1995

41. J.W. McGarvey, *The New Testament Commentary, Vol.I Matthew and Mark*, Delight, Arkansas, Gospel Light Publishing Company, 1875

42. R.T. France, *The Gospel of Matthew*, Grand Rapids, Michigan, WM. B. Eerdmans Publishing Co., 2007

43. Alfred Plummer, *An Exegetical Commentary on the Gospel According to S. Matthew*, Grand Rapids, Michigan, WM. B. Eerdmans Publishing Co., 1956

44. R.T. France, *The Gospel of Matthew*, Grand Rapids, Michigan, WM. B. Eerdmans Publishing Co., 2007

45. J.W. McGarvey, *The New Testament Commentary, Vol. I. Matthew and Mark*, Delight, Arkansas, Gospel Light Publishing Company, 1875

46. Ibid

47. Peter Richardson, *Herod King of the Jews and Friend of the Romans*, Columbia, South Carolina, The University of South Carolina, 1996

48. J.W. McGarvey, *The New Testament Commentary, Vol. I Matthew and Mark*, Delight Arkansas, Gospel Light Publishing Company, 1875

49. R.T. France, *The Gospel of Matthew*, Grand Rapids, Michigan, WM. B. Eerdmans Publishing Co., 2007

50. Henry Dosker, "Herod," *International Standard Bible Encyclopedia*, Grand Rapids, Michigan, WM. B. Eerdmans Publishing Co., 1960

51. William M. Willett, *Herod the Great, The King of the Jews*, Philadelphia, Publication Office at Fetter and Co.'s, 1859

52. Peter Richardson, *Herod King of the Jews and Friend of the Romans*, Columbia, South Carolina, The University of South Carolina, 1996

53. Ibid

54. R.T. France, *The Gospel of Matthew*, Grand Rapids, Michigan, WM. B. Eerdmans Publishing Co., 2007

55. Ibid

56. Ibid

57. J.W. McGarvey, *The New Testament Commentary, Vol. I Matthew and Mark*, Delight, Arkansas, Gospel Light Publishing Company, 1875

58. Leon Morris, *Luke, Tyndale New Testament Commentaries*, Grand Rapids, Michigan, Inter-Varsity Press,, WM. B. Eerdmans Publishing Co.,1999

59. Ibid

60. Louis Sweet, "Mary," *International Standard Bible Encyclopedia*, Grand Rapids, Michigan, WM. B. Eerdmans Publishing Co., 1960

61. Ibid

62. B.F. Westcott, *The Gospel According to St. John*, Grand Rapids, Michigan, WM. B. Eerdmans Publishing Co., 1958

63. Ibid

64. Ibid

65. Louis Sweet, "Mary," *International Standard Bible Encyclopedia*, Grand Rapids, Michigan, WM. B. Eerdmans Publishing Co., 1960

66. B.B. Westcott, *The Gospel According to St. John*, Grand Rapids, Michigan, WM. B. Eerdmans Publishing Co.,1958

67. Louis Sweet, "Mary," *International Bible Encyclopedia*, Grand Rapid, Michigan, WM. B. Eerdmans Publishing Co. 1960

68. F.F. Bruce, *The Acts of the Apostles*, London, The Tyndale Press,1956

69. R.B. Rackham, *The Acts of the Apostles*, London, Methuen and Co. Ltd.,1957

70. H.E. Dana, *The New Testament World*, Nashville, Broadman Press, 1937

About the Author

James Byers is a graduate of David Lipscomb College, magna cum laude, and teaches an Asian Bible class at Harpeth Hills Church of Christ where he serves as a deacon. He has been a minister in congregations in Tennessee, Georgia, Florida, and Hawaii. He had a career with the State of Tennessee as a teacher in Williamson County and with the Department of Human Services. He is married to the former Marie Potter, and they have one son, Tracy Byers, who is married to the former Evie Wade. James and Marie are also proud grandparents of three grandchildren.

Other Titles by This Author

"I have prepared a place for you, in My Father's house where there are many dwelling places" (John 14:2). With these words Jesus encouraged His disciples, and future Christians, of a glorious heaven. His first coming made this hope of heaven possible; His final coming will make it complete.

Hope of Heaven explores some of the expectations and descriptions of heaven throughout the Bible. Christ will come. His eternal kingdom shall be established. This is the great hope and fear of all generations.

"John the Apostle was truly the Christian of the first century. His life spanned the rule of Augustus Caesar through Trajan; thus he lived through the reign of twelve emperors and died during the rule of the thirteenth in the period of time known in Latin as the Pax Romana or Roman peace." (exerpt from first chapter)

The Apostle John: A Blessed Life takes a historical and philosophical look into the life and work of this son of Zebedee. Once a "son of thunder," John's spiritual journey led him to become the man called to write a special, personal account of the life of Jesus. This book guides the reader through the world in which John lived and the Gospel, letters, and revelation tale written with divine direction and his unique perspective.

From his days fishing with his father and brother on the Sea of Galilee, to his travels with Jesus, and finally to his last days writing and sharing Christ's word in Ephesus, this apostle truly lived a blessed life.

www.ingramcontent.com/pod-product-compliance
Lightning Source LLC
LaVergne TN
LVHW050942080826
845145LV00004B/1379

* 9 7 8 0 9 8 6 0 2 4 4 1 2 *